Presented to:

_____

A Gift From:

_____

Date:

_____

also by Jim Coy...

Matthew A to Z + 2 (for adults)

ISBN 978158169-2761

Valor (A Gathering of Eagles Series)

ISBN 158169-1114

Prisoners of Hope (A Gathering of Eagles Series)

ISBN 158169-1777

A Gathering of Eagles II

ISBN 158169-0495

The ABCs of MATTHEW for Kids

Jimmie Coy
and
Patricia Coy Ragsdell

The ABCs of Matthew for Kids
by Jimmie Coy and Patricia Coy Ragsdell
Copyright ©2009 Jimmie Coy and Patricia Coy Ragsdell

ISBN 978-1-58169-318-8
For Worldwide Distribution
Printed in the U.S.A.

Illustrations by Masaru Horie

Evergreen Press
P.O. Box 191540 • Mobile, AL 36619
800-367-8203

Dedication

This book is dedicated to every parent
and grandparent who would like to teach
their children and grandchildren about
the life and teachings of Jesus Christ
using the gospel of Matthew.

Introduction

This book uses the alphabet,
alliteration, and lively illustrations
to help children learn the life
and teachings of
Jesus Christ.

A—Matthew 1

Matthew 1 is the **ANCESTRY** of Jesus from **ABRAHAM** to Jesus. The **ANGEL APPEARED** saying, "Don't be **AFRAID**," and then **ANNOUNCED** Jesus' coming birth and **ARRIVAL**.

B—Matthew 2

The **BABY BOY** would be **BORN** in **BETHLEHEM**. The wise men followed the **BEACON** of light from the **BRIGHT** star. When the wise men and the shepherds saw the **BABY**, they **BOWED** down and worshiped him.

C—Matthew 3

John the Baptist **COULD** be heard **CRYING**, "**CHANGE** your heart." When Jesus was baptized and **CAME** up out of the water, the dove **(COMFORTER) CAME** down from the **CLOUDS**, and a voice was heard saying, "This is my Son."

D—Matthew 4

The **DEVIL DARED** Jesus saying, "If you are **DEITY**, throw yourself **DOWN**. You won't **DASH** your foot." Christ replied, "**DEPART** from me." **DEFEATED** and **DEJECTED**, the **DEVIL DEPARTED**.

E—Matthew 5

The Beatitudes—**EXCITING ETHICS**. The meek will inherit the **EARTH**. You are the **EARTH'S** salt and the light of the world. You have heard it said, "Love your neighbor." I tell you, "Love **EVEN** your **ENEMIES**."

F—Matthew 6

If you will **FORGIVE** other people their **FAILURES**, your heavenly **FATHER** will **FORGIVE** you. Don't worry and **FRET** about the **FUTURE**; the **FUTURE** will take care of itself.

G—Matthew 7

Ask, seek, and knock, and you will **GET. GOD GIVES GOOD GIFTS** to those who ask. Treat other people the way you want to be treated. Live by the **GOLDEN** Rule.

H—Matthew 8

Then **HE HEALED** the centurion's servant who was at **HOME HURTING HORRIBLY. HE** also **HEALED** a man with **HANSEN'S** disease (leprosy) and Peter's mother-in-law of a **HIGH** fever.

I—Matthew 9

Some people brought an **INVALID** man **INSIDE** who was paralyzed, and Jesus said, "Your sins are forgiven." Jesus healed all kinds of **ILLNESSES** and **INFIRMITIES**.

J—Matthew 10

If you will **JUST** acknowledge **JESUS** before men, **JESUS** will acknowledge you before his Father, **JEHOVAH**. "**JUST** give a drink of **JUICE** or water in my name, and you will not lose your reward."

K—Matthew 11

"To enter the **KINGDOM** of heaven, you must **KEEP** the faith. Father, thank you for **KEEPING** these things and this **KNOWLEDGE** from the clever and intelligent, and giving this **KNOWLEDGE** to your children, to your **KIDS**."

L—Matthew 12

The Son of Man is the **LORD** of the Sabbath. Jesus went into the synagogue and healed a man with a **LAME** hand. They asked him, "Is it **LEGAL** to heal on the Sabbath?" He responded, "If you had a **LAMB** and it fell in a ditch, you would **LIFT** it out."

M—Matthew 13

A **MAN** went out to plant seeds. The seeds in good soil
MULTIPLIED MIGHTILY, some by 100, some 60, and some 30.
The seed in good soil is like the **MAN** who hears and understands
the **MESSAGE**. Jesus taught, using **MANY** parables. Some said,
"Where does he get this wisdom? Isn't **MARY** his **MOTHER**?"

N—Matthew 14

After preaching to a large group of people, the disciples said to Jesus, "Send these people away. We have **NO** food." Jesus responded, "There is **NO NEED** to send them away." He then took two fish and five loaves of bread and fed (**NOURISHED**) a crowd that **NUMBERED** 5,000.

A lady came saying, "**OH**, have pity **ON** me. My **ONLY** daughter is terribly sick." He replied, "I was sent **ONLY** to the house of Israel." Then she said, "**OH** Lord, please help. Even the dogs eat by the table of the master." He said, "**OH** woman, you don't lack faith. Your daughter is **OKAY**. She is healed."

P—Matthew 16

Jesus asked, "Who do **PEOPLE** say the Son of Man is?" **PETER** responded, "You are the Christ." Christ told **PETER**, "You are **PETRA**, the rock of the church." Jesus then asked, "What **PROFIT** is it for a man to gain the whole world at the **PRICE** of his soul? What **PRICE** can you **PAY** to **PURCHASE** back your soul?"

Q—Matthew 17

The **QUARTET**, Jesus, Peter, James and his brother, John, went up the high hill. Then His appearance changed before their eyes. His face was like the sun. **QUAKING** with fear, the **QUARTET** heard a **QUOTE** from heaven, saying, "This is my Son in whom I am well pleased."

R—Matthew 18

The disciples came to Jesus with the **RELEVANT** question, "Who is **REALLY** greatest in the kingdom of heaven?" Christ **RESPONDED**, "It is the man who can be as humble as a child who will **REALLY** be the greatest in heaven."

S—Matthew 19

A rich man asked, "How can I **SECURE** eternal life?" Jesus said, "Keep the commandments." The man replied, "I have **SURELY** kept them all." Jesus **SAID**, "**SELL** all you have and give to the poor." **SADLY** the young man left because he was very rich. He had a **SACK** full of **SILVER**.

T—Matthew 20

A farmer hired men to **TOIL** in his field. When **THEY** were paid, **THEY** grumbled saying, "Some of **THESE** last fellows only **TOILED** one hour. You **TREATED THEM** like **THOSE** who **TOILED** all day." The farmer replied, "It is my wish to give the **TARDY** latecomer as much as I gave the first."

U—Matthew 21

Jesus sent two disciples ahead, telling them, "You will find a donkey. **UNTIE** it and bring it **UNTO** me." This fulfilled the Scripture, "Behold the King will come **UNTO** thee, riding **UPON** a donkey." Entering the temple, Jesus was **UPSET** seeing the money changers and turned their tables **UPSIDE** down.

V—Matthew 22

The Pharisees asked him all kinds of **VEXING** questions. One asked, "What is the **VERY** greatest commandment, the most **VALUABLE** commandment?" Jesus replied, "You shall love the Lord thy God with all thy heart, soul, and mind; and the second greatest is love thy neighbor as thyself."

W—Matthew 23

Every man **WHO** promotes himself **WILL** be humbled. **WHOEVER** is **WILLING** to be humble **WILL** be promoted. Christ said, "**WOE** unto you, Scribes and Pharisees. You are hypocrites. You filter out the mosquito, but you swallow the **WHOLE** camel."

X—Matthew 24

You must e**XPECT** his return. The Son of Man will come on clouds in power and splendor. He will send his angels with an e**XTRA** loud trumpet call, and they will gather the chosen. Always be ready and e**XPECT** his return.

Y—Matthew 25

Jesus told his disciples, "Whatever **YOU** did for the **YOUNGEST** of my brothers, **YOU** did for me. Whatever **YOU** failed to do for the **YOUNGEST** of my brothers, **YOU** failed to do for me."

Z—Matthew 26

At the house of Simon, a woman poured expensive perfume on the head of Jesus. The perfume smelled wonderful and was as fresh as a **ZEPHYR**. Seeing this, Judas, acting like a **ZERO**, became angry. Jesus said, "She has done a wonderful thing for me. She is preparing my body for burial."

C2—Matthew 27

When Pilate asked the **CROWD**, "What am I to do with Jesus who is **CALLED CHRIST**," the **CROWD CRIED**, "**CRUCIFY** him!" Pilate said, "But what is his **CRIME?**" Again the **CROWD CRIED**, "**CRUCIFY** him!"

R2—Matthew 28

The angel of the Lord **ROLLED** back the **ROCK**. When Mary went to the tomb, the angel told her, "He is **RISEN**." She **RAN** to tell the disciples that He was **RISEN** and that He was **RESURRECTED**. When the disciples saw Jesus, He said, "Go make disciples. **REMEMBER** I am with you always."

Index & Summary

Glossary

ACKNOWLEDGE, To greet or recognize somebody.

ANCESTRY, Family members who lived a long time ago.

ANNOUNCED, To say something publicly.

BEACON, Bright light used as a signal.

BEATITUDES, Sayings that describe how people should act.

CENTURION, An officer in the ancient Roman army who was in charge of 100 men.

COMFORTER, Person who gives comfort. The Holy Spirit.

COMMANDMENTS, Any of the Ten Commandments, God's laws in the Bible.

DEFEATED, Someone who has lost.

DEITY, God.

DEJECTED, Sad and depressed.

DEPART, To leave.

ETHICS, The way a person behaves.

FAILURES, Not able to do something.

FRET, To worry about something.

FUTURE, The time to come

HYPOCRITE, Someone who pretends to be good.

INFIRMITIES, Weaknesses, sicknesses.

INVALID, A very sick person who can't walk.

JEHOVAH, Hebrew name for God.

LAME, Someone who can't use an arm or a leg.

LEGAL, Allowed by the law.

LEPROSY, A terrible disease.

MESSAGE, The meaning of something.

MULTIPLIED, To cause to increase.

NOURISHED, A person who has enough food to keep them healthy and strong.

PETRA, The Latin word for rock.

PROFIT, To gain or benefit in some way.

QUAKING, Shaking.

QUARTET, Four people.

QUOTE, To repeat words that someone has said.

RELEVANT, Something important to a person.

RESURRECTED, To be raised from the dead.

SABBATH, A day of rest and worship.

SECURE, Safe.

SIGNIFICANT, Important

SORROWFUL, Sad

SOUL, The spiritual part of a person that you can't see.

SYNAGOGUE, A Jewish place of worship.

TOIL, To work hard.

TOMB, A place where dead people are buried.

VEXING, A question that is hard to answer.

WOE, Something that makes you sad or upset.

ZEPHYR, A soft gentle breeze.

ZERO, Slang word for a nobody.

About the Authors

Jim Coy and his wife, Vicki, have three children: Tim, Patricia, and Josh. Jim and Vicki attend New Life Community Church in Columbia, Missouri. They are Associate staff with the Military Ministry of Campus Crusade for Christ.

Patricia Coy Ragsdell and her husband, Keith, live in Virginia and have four children, Jacob, Joseph, Samuel, and Sophia. Patricia has a degree in elementary education and is currently a full-time wife and mother.

To contact the authors:
coyjv@socket.net